C000225690

1,000,000 Books

are available to read at

www.ForgottenBooks.com

Read online
Download PDF
Purchase in print

ISBN 978-0-428-51901-8
PIBN 11303086

This book is a reproduction of an important historical work. Forgotten Books uses
state-of-the-art technology to digitally reconstruct the work, preserving the original format
whilst repairing imperfections present in the aged copy. In rare cases, an imperfection in
the original, such as a blemish or missing page, may be replicated in our edition. We do,
however, repair the vast majority of imperfections successfully; any imperfections that
remain are intentionally left to preserve the state of such historical works.

Forgotten Books is a registered trademark of FB &c Ltd.
Copyright © 2018 FB &c Ltd.
FB &c Ltd, Dalton House, 60 Windsor Avenue, London, SW19 2RR.
Company number 08720141. Registered in England and Wales.

For support please visit www.forgottenbooks.com

1 MONTH OF
FREE
READING

at

www.ForgottenBooks.com

By purchasing this book you are
eligible for one month membership to
ForgottenBooks.com, giving you
unlimited access to our entire
collection of over 1,000,000 titles via
our web site and mobile apps.

To claim your free month visit:

www.forgottenbooks.com/free1303086

* Offer is valid for 45 days from date of purchase. Terms and conditions apply.

English
Français
Deutsche
Italiano
Español
Português

www.forgottenbooks.com

Mythology Photography **Fiction**
Fishing Christianity **Art** Cooking
Essays Buddhism Freemasonry
Medicine **Biology** Music **Ancient
Egypt** Evolution Carpentry Physics
Dance Geology **Mathematics** Fitness
Shakespeare **Folklore** Yoga Marketing
Confidence Immortality Biographies
Poetry **Psychology** Witchcraft
Electronics Chemistry History **Law**
Accounting **Philosophy** Anthropology
Alchemy Drama Quantum Mechanics
Atheism Sexual Health **Ancient History**
Entrepreneurship Languages Sport
Paleontology Needlework Islam
Metaphysics Investment Archaeology
Parenting Statistics Criminology
Motivational

Historic, Archive Document

Do not assume content reflects current
scientific knowledge, policies, or practices.

CIR AERIAL PHOTOS

92131

CONTENTS

Report No. 87-1

3400
December 1986

$2\overset{\curlywedge}{4}\overset{\curlyvee}{5}$ IDENTIFICATION OF RED SPRUCE AND FRASER FIR
ON LARGE SCALE CIR AERIAL PHOTOS

by

W.M. Ciesla, E.T. Wilson, B.B. Eav, and J.D. Ward[1/2/]
USDA Forest Service

ABSTRACT

Ability to identify red spruce, Picea rubens, and Fraser fir, Abies fraseri, on large scale color infrared (CIR) aerial photos was evaluated for a site on Roan Mountain, a high peak on the North Carolina-Tennessee border. Overall classification accuracy for two experienced photo interpreters and several combinations of crown closure, photo scale, and IR balance was 72.1 percent. Classification accuracies varied slightly by crown closure, photo scale, and IR balance, but differences were not statistically significant (p=0.10). Red spruce and Fraser fir were also classified into two condition classes; healthy and "declining", on 1:2000 scale CIR photos, with 60 percent accuracy. Characteristics used to separate the two species and classify them into condition classes are described.

INTRODUCTION

Recent reports of decline and mortality of red spruce, Picea rubens, in the spruce-fir forests of eastern North America has led to the conduct of special inventories to determine its extent and probable causes (Weiss and others 1985; Mielke and others 1986). Color infrared (CIR) aerial photography has been used in these inventories to identify vegetation communities with a

[1/] The authors are respectively, Group Leader, Forest Pest Management/Methods Application Group, Fort Collins, CO; formerly Biological Technician, Doraville Field Office, Forest Pest Management, Southern Region, Doraville, GA, presently retired and residing in Albuquerque, NM; Operations Research Analyst, Forest Pest Management/Methods Application Group, Fort Collins, CO; and Supervisory Entomologist, Doraville Field Office, Forest Pest Management, Southern Region, Doraville, GA;

[2/] Partial funding for this work was provided by the USDA Forest Service, Southeastern Forest Experiment Station Atmospheric Deposition/Vegetation Survey RD&A Program located at the Forestry Sciences Laboratory, Research Triangle Park, NC.

spruce-fir component and as an intermediate sampling stage for estimating levels of tree mortality (Ciesla and others 1986).

Forest declines have been recently been reported on commercially important tree species in central Europe (Schutt and Cowling 1985), and CIR aerial photography has been used to inventory the status of these declines in West Germany and other western European nations (Hildebrandt and Kadro 1984). An approach used in the European inventories is to classify the full range of decline symptoms on the aerial photos. This requires that photo interpreters have the ability to identify tree species and classify the various symptoms of decline consistently and reliably. Workers in West Germany have developed guides to aid in species identification and decline rating on large scale CIR aerial photos (Grundmann 1984; Masumy 1984).

Tree species identification on true color or panchromatic aerial photos in North America is reviewed by Heller and others (1964); Parry and others (1969); and Sayn-Wittgenstein (1978). Other than broad recognition of species groups (i.e., conifers versus hardwoods) only a limited amount of information is available on tree species identification in North America on CIR film. Ciesla (1984) prepared general guidelines for identification of conifers indigenous to the northeastern United States on CIR film in support of an inventory of decline and mortality in red spruce and balsam fir, Abies balsamea, in New Hampshire, New York, and Vermont (Weiss and others 1985). These guides were based on the same characteristics of crown shape, apex, margin, and foliage texture used for species identification with panchromatic or color aerial photos.

Recently one of the authors (E.T. Wilson) observed distinct color differences between red spruce and Fraser fir, A. fraseri, when interpreting CIR photos taken in the southern Appalachian Mountains. Red spruce tended to appear in hues of red brown or red violet, whereas Fraser fir was typically a dark red hue. In West Germany, similar color differences plus textural characteristics of the foliage are routinely used to separate Norway spruce, P. abies, from silver fir, A. alba, on large scale CIR aerial photos (Grundmann 1984).

This paper reports results of an evaluation to determine if red spruce and Fraser fir could be reliability separated on large scale CIR photos using characteristics of crown form, foliage texture, and color. The evaluation also provided an opportunity to determine if certain decline symptoms could also be detected and classified.

METHODS

The evaluation was designed to compare effects of photo interpreter, scale, crown closure, and IR balance on the ability to distinguish between red spruce and Fraser fir.

4

EVALUATION SITE

The evaluation site is located on Roan Mountain in Mitchell County, North Carolina, and Carter County, Tennessee. Roan Mountain consists of a pair of peaks on the dividing ridge which separates North Carolina and Tennessee. The two peaks, Roan High Bluff and Roan High Knob, reach elevations of 6,267 and 6,285 feet, respectively. Most of the site is on National Forest land; the North Carolina portion is part of the Pisgah National Forest and the Tennessee portion is part of the Cherokee National Forest.

Roan Mountain is one of six major areas of native red spruce-Fraser fir forest in the southern Appalachian Mountains. There are approximately 1,537 acres of spruce-fir type in this area, extending from a lower elevational limit of approximately 5,000 feet to the summits of the two peaks. The spruce-fir forest is interspersed by a series of grassy areas locally known as balds and extensive "gardens" of Catawba rhododendron, Rhododendron catawbiense, Michx. Associated hardwoods include yellow birch, Betula alleghaniensis, Britton, and American mountain ash, Sorbus americana, Marsh. A mixed northern hardwood forest occupies the slopes at elevations below the lower elevational limits of the spruce-fir type.

The balsam woolly adelgid, Adelges piceae, Ratzburg, a stem and branch infesting adelgid of true firs introduced into North America from Europe, was discovered on Roan Mountain in 1962 (Ciesla and Buchanan 1962). This insect has caused extensive mortality of the Fraser fir component of most of the spruce-fir forests in the southern Appalachian Mountains, including Roan Mountain, since the late 1950's.

AERIAL PHOTOGRAPHY

Existing CIR transparencies of Roan Mountain, originally acquired to document the progression of tree mortality caused by balsam woolly adelgid and photography acquired specifically for this project was used in this evaluation. All photography was taken by the USDA Forest Service, Southern Region, Forest Pest Management Field Office, Doraville, Georgia. A Wild RC-10[3]/ 9X9 inch aerial camera equipped with a 6-inch focal length lens was used for all photo missions.

Photography was acquired from April 1982 through September 1985 and included three photo scales; 1:2000, 1:4000, and 1:8000. Two sets of 1:4000 scale photos were available, one with a normal IR balance, and one with an enhanced IR balance giving the film an excessive red color. The IR balance of the 1:2000 and 1:8000 photos was also excessively red.

PHOTO INTERPRETATION

Sample trees were selected, marked, and numbered on each set of photos. Trees in two stand conditions were included. These were open stands where the crown closure was less than 75 percent and the crown margin of each tree was

---

[3]/Mention of commercial names is for convenience only and does not imply endorsement by USDA Forest Service.

clearly visible, and closed stands, where crown closure was equal to or in excess of 75 percent and all or a portion of the crown margin of sample trees was obscured by neighboring trees. Only trees which could be readily located on the ground were selected for classification.

Two experienced photo interpreters, familiar with the target site, independently examined each tree in stereo and classified it as a spruce or fir. Characteristics used to separate spruce from fir included foliage color, texture, crown shape, apex and margin. Descriptions provided by Parry and others (1969), and Sayn-Wittgenstein (1978) for red spruce, white spruce, P. glauca and balsam fir, coupled with preliminary observations by the photo interpreters were used to develop classification standards (Figure 1, Table 1). Since foliage color of individual trees is influenced by film exposure, IR balance, vignetting, and sun angle in addition to species, only relative color differences were used to aid in species classification. Standard Munsell color chips were used for descriptive purposes only and not in the actual classification procedure (Anon 1976). A total of 409 trees were classified on the aerial photos (Table 2).

During the tree species identification procedure, sample trees with sparse foliage and bare branches were noted. Following completion of the photo interpretation for species identification, one photo interpreter classified all sample trees on the 1:2000 scale photos into two tree condition classes:

> Healthy - More than 90 percent of the crown area with apparently
>   healthy foliage.
>
> Declining - 10 percent or more of the crown area with foliage missing.
>   and bare branches distinctly visible.

GROUND DATA

An attempt was made to locate all of the trees classified on the aerial photos on the ground during May 1986 and record the species. Tree condition class was also recorded for trees classified on the 1:2000 scale photos. A total of 228 trees (64 red spruce, 164 Fraser fir) or 56 percent of the trees classified on the photos were located and classified on the ground (Table 2).

DATA ANALYSIS

For the tree species identification, aerial photo and corresponding ground data for each combination of photo scale, photo interpreter, IR balance, and crown closure was summarized in 2X2 error matrices. The measure of agreement $\hat{K}$ and its variance was computed for each error matrix using procedures described by Bishop et al. (1975). Differences between $\hat{K}$ values for various combinations of photo scale, IR balance, and crown closure were tested by using the discrete multivariate analysis procedures developed for error matrices described by Congalton et al. (1983).

Tree species and condition class data from the 1:2000 scale photos was summarized into a 4X4 error matrix and a test was conducted to determine if differences in agreement occurred between open and closed stands.

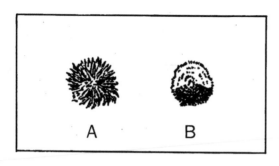

ral appearance of red spruce and Fraser fir on large scale CIR
ial photos: A. Red spruce; B. Fraser fir.

ary of foliar and crown characteristics used to distinguish red
e from Fraser fir on large scale color-IR aerial photos, Roan
tain, North Carolina and Tennessee.

tic	: : :	Red Spruce	: : :	Fraser Fir
		Dark red brown or red violet.		Dark red.
e		Coarse, branches distinctly visible, radiating from main-stem in a starlike pattern.		Fine and compact, branches usually not distinctly visible.
		Broadly conical.		Narrowly conical.
		Obtuse, crown tip not distinct.		Acute or acuminate, crown tip distinct, often high-lighted by a white or silvery hue.
		Lobed to deeply serrate.		Finely serrate.

Table 2 - Number of red spruce and Fraser fir classified on aerial photos and on the ground by photo scale and stand condition, Roan Mountain, North Carolina and Tennessee.

Scale	Number of Frames	Stand Condition	Number of Trees Classified	
			Aerial Photos	Ground
·1:2000	3	Open	69	50
		Closed	36	30
1:4000 (IR normal)	4	Open	77	43
		Closed	27	7
1:4000 (IR enhanced)	3	Open	81	47
		Closed	15	9
1:8000	4	Open	71	21
		Closed	33	21
All Scales	14	Open	298	161
		Closed	111	67
		Total	409	228

RESULTS

QUALITY OF AERIAL PHOTOS

Overall photo quality was less than optimum. Three of the four sets of photos had an enhanced IR balance. This caused an intensification of the red tones and reduced subtle contrasts between the red hues normally used to identify vegetation types on CIR film. The one set of photos with a normal IR balance was slightly underexposed, had long shadows, and the hardwoods were in a leaf-off condition. These were taken at a time of year when aerial photos would not normally be acquired for forest damage assessment (Table 3).

CHARACTERISTICS OF RED SPRUCE AND FRASER FIR ON CIR PHOTOS

FOLIAGE COLOR - Slight differences in foliage color between red spruce and Fraser fir were noted by the photo interpreters, thus confirming the earlier observations. These proved helpful in separating the two species. Under conditions of optimum exposure, red spruce tends to have a distinct red-brown hue and Fraser fir more of a dark red hue similar to that reported for Norway spruce and silver fir in West Germany (Grundmann 1984). These color contrasts are less distinct on CIR photos with an enhanced IR balance (Table 4).

Tree age and size also tends to influence foliage color. Pure stands of young sapling size Fraser fir had a more intense chroma than did their larger, older counterparts. An insufficient number of sapling size red spruce were

8

Table 3 - Characteristics of CIR photos used to identify red spruce and Fraser fir, Roan Mountain, North Carolina and Tennessee.

Targeted Photo Scale	Actual Photo Scale	Date of Photography	IR Balance	Condition of Hardwood Foliage
1:2000	1:2779	28 Sep 85	Enhanced	Leaf on - early fall coloring
1:4000	1:4830	28 Sep 85	Enhanced	Leaf on - early fall coloring
1:4000	1:4652	1 Apr 82	Normal	Leaf off
1:8000	1:8640	Jul 84	Slightly Enhanced	Leaf on

Table 4 - Munsell color descriptions for red spruce and Fraser fir on CIR aerial film, Roan Mountain, North Carolina and Tennessee[1].

Species	IR Normal			IR Enhanced		
	Value	Hue	Chroma	Value	Hue	Chroma
Red Spruce	5R	3	4	5R	4	6,8
Fraser Fir	5R	4	8	5R	4	10,12

[1]Color descriptions are for large open grown trees on optimally exposed portions of photos.

observed to enable us to determine if this species has a similar color pattern. Grundmann (1984) reports that in West Germany, young, sapling size Norway spruce are a brighter, lighter red color than their older counterparts.

FOLIAGE AND BRANCH TEXTURE - Red spruce has distinct branches radiating from the mainstem in a starlike pattern regardless of tree age or size. Foliage and branch texture of Fraser fir, on the other hand, tends to change slightly with tree size, age, and exposure to severe weather. Young trees typically have the same smooth textured foliage and indistinct branches reported in the literature for balsam fir (Parry and others 1969; Sayn-Wittgenstein 1978). As trees get older and larger they develop a branch

9

texture which looks much like an inverted pine cone and makes them less easily separable from red spruce.

CROWN FORM - Fraser fir has essentially the same overall crown form as does balsam fir; an acute or acuminate crown apex with a distinct crown tip (Parry and others 1969; Sayn-Wittgenstein 1978). Again, this characteristic is more visible on smaller, younger trees. The crown tip is also frequently highlighted by a white or silvery patch. In red spruce the crown apex is more obtuse and the crown tip is not as distinct.

ABILITY TO SEPARATE RED SPRUCE FROM FRASER FIR

PHOTO INTERPRETERS - Photo interpreters were remarkably consistent in their classification. Photo interpreter 1 had an overall classification accuracy of 71.5 percent; and photo interpreter 2 had an overall classification accuracy of 72.8 percent; a net difference of three trees. Classification accuracy decreased slightly with a corresponding decrease in scale (Table 5).

Statistical comparison of photo interpreters classification accuracy for each combination of photo scale, IR balance, and crown closure showed no significant differences (Table 6). Therefore data for both photo interpreters was combined and treated as independent observations in all subsequent tests (Table 7). Five of the eight resultant error matrices had correct classifications significantly greater than what could be expected by pure chance (>50% p = <.10) (Table 8).

CROWN CLOSURE - Comparison of the ability to separate the two species by crown closure class indicated that there was essentially no difference. A significant difference did occur in the crown closure classes for the 1:4000 IR enhanced photo scale (Table 9). The significance of this difference, however, is questionable due to the relatively small number of trees (N=18) in the closed crown condition class (Table 7).

PHOTO SCALE AND IR BALANCE - There was no significant difference in ability to separate red spruce from Fraser fir for the photo scale used in this evaluation. In addition, at a scale of 1:4000, IR balance had no significant effect on ability to classify these species (Table 10).

DAMAGE RATING

SYMPTOMS - The predominant type of damage observed on living trees on the aerial photos was areas of grey discoloration in the interior of the crown. This was suggestive of a loss of older foliage and branch dieback.

Ground observations confirmed that individual trees did have less than the normal compliment of older foliage. On Roan Mountain, vigorous, apparently healthy red spruce and Fraser fir normally retain five to six years of foliage. Trees with a "decline" syndrome only retain two to three years of foliage giving the crown an open, tufted apprearance.

10

Table 5 - Error matrices for classification of red spruce and Fraser fir on large scale color-IR aerial photos by scale, IR balance, crown closure class and photo interpreter, Roan Mountain, North Carolina and Tennessee.

Scale	Crown Closure Class		Aerial Photo Classification							
			PI-1				PI-2			
			Spruce	Fir	Total	% Correct	Spruce	Fir	Total	% Correct
1:2000	Open	Spruce	12	3	15	80.0	12	3	15	80.0
		Fir	6	29	35	82.9	8	27	35	77.1
		Total	18	32	50	82.0	20	30	50	78.0
	Closed	Spruce	1	7	8	12.5	3	5	8	37.3
		Fir	0	22	22	100.0	2	20	22	90.9
		Total	1	29	30	76.7	5	25	30	76.7
1:4000 (IR normal)	Open	Spruce	9	1	10	90.0	8	2	10	80.0
		Fir	15	18	33	54.5	15	18	33	54.5
		Total	24	19	43	62.8	23	20	43	60.5
	Closed	Spruce	0	0	0	--	0	0	0	--
		Fir	4	3	7	42.9	3	4	7	57.1
		Total	4	3	7	42.9	3	4	7	57.1
1:4000 (IR enhanced)	Open	Spruce	10	6	16	62.5	11	5	16	68.8
		Fir	10	21	31	67.7	7	24	31	77.4
		Total	20	27	47	65.9	18	29	47	74.5
	Closed	Spruce	2	1	3	66.7	3	0	3	66.7
		Fir	0	6	6	100.0	0	6	6	100.0
		Total	2	7	9	88.8	3	6	9	100.0
1:8000	Open	Spruce	4	2	6	66.7	3	3	6	50.0
		Fir	5	10	15	66.7	4	11	15	73.3
		Total	9	12	21	66.7	7	14	21	66.7
	Closed	Spruce	4	2	6	66.7	4	2	6	66.7
		Fir	3	12	15	80.0	3	12	15	80.0
		Total	7	14	21	76.2	7	14	21	76.2
Overall % correct			163/228 -			71.5	166/228 -			72.8

GROUND DATA

11

Table 6 - Summary of tests comparing ability of two photo interpreters to identify red spruce and Fraser fir on various combinations of photo scale, IR balance, and crown closure, Roan Mountain, North Carolina and Tennessee.

Photo Scale	Crown Closure Class	Photo Interpreter				Z Statistic	Significance Level
		PI 1		PI 2			
		$\hat{K}$	Var $(\hat{K})$	$\hat{K}$	Var $(\hat{K})$		
1:2000	Open	.595	.015	.522	.016	.416	.677 NS[1]
	Closed	.173	.086	.323	.044	.416	.678 NS
1:4000 (IR Normal)	Open	.299	.029	.238	.032	.248	.804 NS
	Closed	.000	.571	.000	.571	.000	.999 NS
1:4000 (IR Enhanced)	Open	.285	.021	.448	.018	.821	.412 NS
	Closed	.727	.064	1.000	.000	1.080	.280 NS
1:8000	Open	.290	.051	.222	.051	.212	.832 NS
	Closed	.444	.045	.444	.045	.000	.999 NS

[1] NS - Not Significant at $p \leq .10$
    S - Significant   at $p \leq .10$

12

Table 7 - Error matrices for classification of red spruce and Fraser fir on large scale CIR photos by scale, IR balance, and crown color, for combined photo interpreters, Roan Mountain, North Carolina and Tennessee.

Scale	Ground Data Crown Closure Class	Species	Aerial Photo Classification Spruce	Fir	Total	% Correct
1:2000	Open	Spruce	24	6	30	80.0
		Fir	14	56	70	80.0
		Total	38	62	100	80.0
	Closed	Spruce	4	12	16	25.0
		Fir	2	42	44	95.5
		Total	6	54	60	76.7
1:4000 (IR normal)	Open	Spruce	17	3	20	85.0
		Fir	30	36	66	54.5
		Total	47	39	86	61.6
	Closed	Spruce	0	0	0	--
		Fir	7	7	14	50.0
		Total	7	7	14	50.0
1:4000 (IR enhanced)	Open	Spruce	21	11	32	65.6
		Fir	17	45	62	72.6
		Total	38	56	94	70.2
	Closed	Spruce	5	1	6	83.3
		Fir	0	12	12	100.0
		Total	5	13	18	94.4
1:8000 (IR enhanced)	Open	Spruce	7	5	12	58.3
		Fir	9	21	30	70.0
		Total	16	26	42	66.7
	Closed	Spruce	8	4	12	66.7
		Fir	6	24	30	80.0
		Total	14	28	42	76.2
	Overall % correct				326/456 = 72.1	

13

Table 8 - $\hat{K}$ values of combined photo interpreters for red spruce and Fras
Fraser fir classification on various combinations of scale,
balance, and crown closure, Roan Mountain, North Carolina a
Tennessee.

Photo Scale	Crown Closure Class	$\hat{K}$	Var $(\hat{K})$	Significance Level[1]
1:2000	Open	.558	.008	.000 S
	Closed	.225	.028	.129 NS
1:4000 IR Normal	Open	.269	.015	.030 S
	Closed	.000	.286	.999 NS
1:4000 IR Enhanced	Open	.365	.010	.080 S
	Closed	.870	.016	.000 S
1:8000	Open	.257	.025	.106 NS
	Closed	.444	.022	.003 S

[1]NS - Not Significant at $P \leq .10$
   S - Significant   at $P \leq .10$

Table 9 - Summary of tests comparing ability to identify red spruce and Fr
fir on CIR photos by crown closure class on various combination
scale and IR balance, Roan Mountain, North Carolina and Tennesse

Photo Scale	Crown Closure Class				Z Statistic	Significa Level[1]
	Open		Closed			
	$\hat{K}$	Var $(\hat{K})$	$\hat{K}$	Var $(\hat{K})$		
1:2000	.558	.008	.255	.028	1.60	.111 N
1:4000 (IR Normal)	.269	.015	.000	.286	0.49	.624 N
1:4000 (IR Enhanced)	.365	.010	.870	.016	3.14	.002 S
1:8000	.258	.025	.444	.022	0.87	.392 N

[1]NS - Not Significant at $p \leq 0.10$
   S - Significant   at $p \leq 0.10$

Table 10 - Summary of tests comparing ability to classify red spruce and
Fraser fir by various combinations of photo scale and IR balance
Roan Mountain, North Carolina and Tennessee.

Test $\hat{K}_1$ vs $\hat{K}_2$	$\hat{K}_1$	Var $(\hat{K})_1$	$\hat{K}_2$	Var $(\hat{K})_2$	Z Statistic	Significance Level[1]
1:2000 vs 1:4000 (IR Enhanced)	.475	.006	.440	.008	.291	.771 NS
1:2000 vs 1:8000	.475	.006	.349	.012	.938	.348 NS
1:4000 vs 1:8000 (IR Enhanced)	.440	.008	.349	.012	.651	.515 NS
1:4000 vs 1:4000 (Enhanced) (Normal)	.440	.008	.237	.015	1.350	.177 NS

[1]/NS - Not Significant at $p \leq .10$
S - Significant at $p \leq .10$

Fraser fir displayed this symptom most frequently. Foliage loss was
usually accompanied by branch dieback and branchlets being turned downward at
the ends (Figure 2). These types of damage are associated with twig and
branch infestations of balsam woolly adelgid (Balch 1952). This insect is
known to be generally distributed throughout the Fraser fir on Roan Mountain.

Red spruce occassionally also displayed a loss of older foliage. Trees
which displayed this symptom were primarily large, overmature trees growing on
steep rocky slopes exposed to high winds. Some trees also had top kill, the
cause of which is presently unknown (Figure 3).

ABILITY TO CLASSIFY DAMAGE - Ability of a single photo interpreter to
classify red spruce and Fraser fir into two damage classes; healthy and
declining, on 1:2000 scale CIR photos was compared for the two crown closure
classes. Classification accuracy was 62 percent ($\hat{K}$=.416) for open stands and
56.7 percent ($\hat{K}$=.260) for closed stands (Table 11). These differences were
not significant at the 0.10 level when compared statistically (Z=.831,
significance level = .404).

15

Figure 2 - Healthy and "declining" Fraser fir: A. Young vigorous tree (1) contrasted with trees classified as "declining" (2). Note tufted branches caused by loss of older foliage. B. Fraser fir in final stages of decline due to infestation of balsam woolly adelgid (1). Note how ends of branches are turned downward. A young vigorous fir occurs in the background (2).

16

Figure 3 — A. An apparently healthy, vigorous red spruce. B. Large, overmature red spruce with tufted foliage, an open crown, and top kill. This tree was growing on a steep, rocky slope exposed to high winds.

17

Table 11 - Error matrices for classification of red spruce and Fraser fir by damage class on 1:2000 scale CIR aerial photos, Roan Mountain, North Carolina and Tennessee.

Crown Closure Class	Ground Data — Species	Condition Class	Aerial Photo Classification				Total	% Correct
			Spruce Healthy	Spruce Declining	Fir Healthy	Fir Declining		
Open	Spruce	Healthy	6	5	2	0	13	47.2
		Declining	0	1	0	0	1	100.0
	Fir	Healthy	3	2	22	0	27	81.5
		Declining	2	3	2	2	9	22.2
	Total		11	11	26	2	50	62.0
Closed	Spruce	Healthy	1	0	5	0	6	16.7
		Declining	0	1	0	0	1	100.0
	Fir	Healthy	1	0	14	0	15	93.0
		Declining	0	2	5	1	8	12.5
	Total		2	3	24	1	30	56.7
Combined	Spruce	Healthy	7	5	7	0	19	36.8
		Declining	0	2	0	0	2	100.0
	Fir	Healthy	4	2	36	0	42	85.7
		Declining	2	5	7	3	17	17.6
	Total		13	14	50	3	80	60.0

DISCUSSION AND CONCLUSIONS

Differences in foliage color, crown form, and foliage and branch texture on large scale CIR aerial photos of red spruce and Fraser fir in the southern Appalachian Mountains were not as distinct as those reported for similar species in West Germany. However, the photo interpretation standards used in this evaluation permitted two experienced photo interpreters to identify the two species correctly in about three out of four cases. Classification accuracies varied slightly by crown closure class, photo scale, and IR balance; however, under conditions of this evaluation, these variations were not statistically significant.

Similarly, at a photo scale of 1:2000, red spruce and Fraser fir could be classified into two broad damage classes; healthy and declining, with about 60 percent accuracy. It is not practical to consistently achieve this large a scale of aerial photography with a conventional mapping camera over large areas however, because the film cannot consistently recycle in sufficient time to acquire the 60-70 percent overlap required for stereo viewing. Therefore, future work on species identification and damage classification should be focused on photo scales of 1:4000 - 1:8000.

The major factor which introduced error into the tree species classification was the appearance of a more distinct branching pattern on the large, dominant, Fraser fir. These were frequently misclassified as red spruce. In addition, the abundance of damage symptoms associated with twig and branch infestations of the balsam woolly adelgid on Fraser fir was unexpected. This also resulted in the misclassification of many Fraser fir as red spruce. Historically, stem or bole infestations of this insect, which cause a rapid death of the host tree, have been the characteristic form of attack in the southern Appalachian Mountains. Presently the twig or branch form of attack appears to be equally prevalent on Roan Mountain.

Ideally, classification accuracies for both tree species and damage classes should be about 90 percent. By using the additional data acquired from this evaluation to redefine photo interpretation standards and exposing CIR film with a normal IR balance, it may be possible to achieve that level of classification accuracy in the future. Additional work is planned to refine and further evaluate these procedures.

ACKNOWLEDGMENTS

Thanks are extended to C.W. Dull and Walt Salazar, USDA Forest Service, Doraville, Georgia, for their assistance with the collection of ground data. A special thanks is extended to Walt Salazar for serving as chief cook during the four day encampment on Roan Mountain during which the ground data were acquired.

C.W. Dull and Walt Salazar also provided constructive comments in the preparation of this manuscript as did W.H. Clerke, Remote Sensing Specialist, Engineering Staff, USDA Forest Service, Southern Region, Atlanta, GA.

LITERATURE CITED

Anonymous. 1976. Munsell book of color - matte finish collection. Munsell Color, MacBeth a Div. of Kollmorgen Corp., Baltimore, MD.

Balch, R.E. 1952. Studies of the balsam woolly aphid, *Adelges piceae* (Ratz) and its effects on balsam fir, *Abies balsamea* (L.) Mill. Dept. Agr. Canada Pub. 867, 76 pp.

Bishop, Y., S. Feinberg, and P. Holland. 1975. Discrete multivariate analysis - theory and practice. MIT Press:Cambridge, MA, 575 pp.

Ciesla, W.M. 1984. Cooperative survey of red spruce and balsam fir decline in New Hampshire, New York, and Vermont - 1984, photo interpretation guidelines. USDA Forest Service, Forest Pest Management, Methods Application Group, Fort Collins, CO, 29 pp.

Ciesla, W.M. and W.D. Buchanan. 1962. Biological evaluation of balsam woolly aphid, Roan Mountain Gardens - Toecane District, Pisgah National Forest - North Carolina. USDA Forest Service Division of State and Private Forestry, Atlanta, GA. Report No. 62-93, 3 pp.

Ciesla, W.M., C.W. Dull, L.R. McCreery, and M.E. Mielke. 1986. Inventory of decline and mortality in spruce-fir forests of the eastern United States with CIR photos. Proceedings ISPRS Comm. VII; Aug. 24-29, 1986. Enschede, the Netherlands.

Congalton, R.G., R.G. Oderwald, and R.A. Mead. 1983. Assessing landsat classification accuracy using discrete multivariate analysis statistical techniques. *Photogrammetric Engineering and Remote Sensing* 49:1671-1678.

Grundmann, O. 1984. Zur Aufstellung von Interpretationschlüsseln für die Schadeinstufung von Fichte und Tanne in Infrarot-Farbbildern. *Allgem. Forst Zeits.* 39(43/44):1093-1094.

Heller, R.C., G.E. Doverspike, and R.C. Aldrich. 1964. Identification of tree species on large-scale panchromatic and color aerial photographs. USDA Forest Service, Agri. Handb. 261, 17 pp.

Hildebrandt, G. and A. Kadro. 1984. Aspects of countrywide inventory and monitoring of actual forest damages in Germany. Bildmessung und Luftbild-wesen. 52:201-216.

Masumy, S. 1984. Interpretationsschüssel zur Auswertung von Infrarot-Farbluftbildern für die Waldschadensinventur. *Allgem. Forst Zeits.* 39:1093-1094.

Mielke, M.E., D.G. Soctomah, M.A. Marsden, and W.M. Ciesla. 1986. Decline and mortality of red spruce in West Virginia. USDA Forest Service, Forest Pest Management, Methods Application Group, Fort Collins, CO. Report No. 86-4, 26 pp.

Parry, J.T., W.R. Cowan, and J.A. Heginbottom. 1969. Color for coniferous species. Photogrammetric Engineering 34:669-678.

Sayn-Wittgenstein, L. 1978. Recognition of tree species on aerial photographs. Canadian Forestry Service, Department of the Environment, Forest Management Institute, Ottawa. Information Report FMR-X-118, 97 pp.

Schutt, P. and E.B. Cowling. 1985. Waldsterben, a general decline of forests in central Europe: symptoms, development and probable causes. Plant Disease 69:1-9.

Weiss, M.J., L.R. McCreery, I. Millers, M. Miller-Weeks, and J.T. O'Brien. 1985. Cooperative survey of red spruce and balsam fir decline and mortality in New York, Vermont, and New Hampshire. USDA Forest Service, Northeastern Area, Broomall, PA, 53 pp.

CPSIA information can be obtained
at www.ICGtesting.com
Printed in the USA
BVHW08s1102170918
527713BV00021B/582/P